Sara's Friends

mactracks

Sara's Friends

Rosina Umelo

mactracks

© Copyright text Rosina Umelo 1993
© Copyright illustrations The Macmillan Press Ltd 1993

All rights reserved. No reproduction, copy or transmission of
this publication may be made without written permission.

No paragraph of this publication may be reproduced, copied or
transmitted save with written permission or in accordance with
the provisions of the Copyright, Designs and Patents Act 1988,
or under the terms of any licence permitting limited copying issued
by the Copyright Licensing Agency, 90 Tottenham Court Road,
London W1P 9HE.

Any person who does any unauthorised act in relation to this
publication may be liable to criminal prosecution and civil claims
for damages.

First published 1993

Published by THE MACMILLAN PRESS LTD
London and Basingstoke
*Associated companies and representatives in Accra,
Auckland, Delhi, Dublin, Gaborone, Hamburg, Harare,
Hong Kong, Kuala Lumpur, Lagos, Manzini, Melbourne,
Mexico City, Nairobi, New York, Singapore, Tokyo.*

ISBN 0-333-60213-7

Printed in Hong Kong

A catalogue record for this book is available from the
British Library.

Series editor: Lorna Evans

Illustrations by Ann Gowland

Chapter 1

"Has anyone seen Sara?" asked Rachel.

The last few weeks of the long school holiday had been very busy for everyone in the class. Rachel went to stay with her mother's sister, to help her get ready for a wedding in the family. Jacob worked with his father. Debora's mother had a new baby. Daniel went to the coast with his father to buy dried fish for the market. Kipi worked with his brother in his mechanic's shed.

Suddenly it was time for school again. Everyone in the school compound was shouting and laughing. When they went to the classroom, they were still almost as noisy. This was the time to look around, meet friends and share news.

The five friends found desks near to each other in their new classrooms. They sat down and talked as loudly as all the others.

"Where's Sara?" asked Jacob. "Let's keep a place for her ... Sorry," he said to a boy who had just arrived, "This place is for Sara."

"Where is she? Sara isn't usually late."

"Do you think she'll be in this class?" Kipi asked. "You know she missed the exam at the end of term."

Rachel was watching the door. The teacher must be arriving soon. "Surely she will," she said. "I know she passed the mid-year exam very well. Sara's clever."

"But she was away from school at the end of the year," Kipi went on. "She might have to repeat a class."

"We've all been together for so long," Debora added. "It won't be the same without Sara."

"I'll look for her next door." Jacob went to the classroom where they had been last term. He looked around. He saw many faces he knew well, and a few new ones too. Sara was not there.

He went back to his own classroom. "That's strange!" he said, frowning.

"She'll look for us as soon as she comes in," said Rachel hopefully.

Daniel began to tell them about his travels. He was in the middle

of an exciting story about a storm and a leaking canoe when the door opened.

"Hush! Hush!" hissed everybody.

The teacher came in. There was still no sign of Sara. The teacher called the roll for the first time in the new school year. He did not call Sara's name. He sent another student to the empty desk the friends were still trying to save for her.

The friends looked at each other. What had happened to Sara?

The long first morning went on. Everyone wrote down the timetable. The class chose Jacob to be the class prefect as usual. The teacher reminded everyone that this was a senior class. They were

expected to work hard and set a good example to other students. It was just like any first day of the school year.

When the bell rang for break, everyone hurried outside. Jacob stopped when he saw Mr Buah. He had been their class teacher last term.

"Good morning, Sir. Please, can you tell me if Sara is in your class this year?"

"Hallo, Jacob. How did you enjoy your holiday? No, Sara isn't in my class."

"We haven't seen her yet. We don't know where she is."

"The Principal told me she isn't coming back to school."

"She's dropped out?" Jacob couldn't believe it.

"I know Sara isn't the kind of girl to drop out," the teacher agreed. "But I heard she's ill. That's why she's left school."

"But . . . but people don't leave school because they're ill," said Jacob. "They stay at home until they feel better, then they come back."

"That depends on what's wrong with them," said the teacher, moving away.

Jacob went out into the compound. Big trees shaded parts of it from the hot sun. His friends were waiting for him.

"What did he say?"

"He said Sara's left school because she's ill. Did anyone see her during the holidays?"

"I did," said Debora. "I went to tell her we had a new baby. That was the day the holidays began."

"I did too," said Rachel. "I went to tell her I was going to stay with Auntie. It was about a week after school closed."

"That's quite a long time ago. Was she ill then?"

"I – I'm not sure. She said she had a bad headache."

"That's what she kept saying last term," put in Debora, "Before she stopped coming to school."

"She said her eyes hurt," added Rachel. "She was lying down with a wet cloth over her face."

"Perhaps she had fever," suggested Daniel. "That's what Mama does for us when we have fever."

"I don't *think* she had fever," said Rachel. "She just said the sunshine hurt her eyes. She seemed very sad."

"It might have been measles," said Kipi. "Did she have any spots?"

Rachel shook her head. "I asked Mama Sara what was the matter. She just said, 'I don't know.'"

"But people don't usually leave school because they're sad – or even because they're ill." Daniel said what they were all thinking.

"It depends what's wrong with them. That's what Mr Buah said." Jacob frowned.

"What could be serious enough to stop Sara from coming to school?" asked Rachel. "She likes it so much."

The bell ringer came out on to the verandah and began to swing the heavy brass handbell.

"Please try to go and see her this afternoon," said Jacob to the two girls. "We have to find out what's wrong."

Later that afternoon Rachel told her mother all about the first day in the new class. "Everyone was there except Sara," she explained. "May I go to her house and find out what's wrong?"

"Be quick then," her mother said, and Rachel hurried off. On the way she called at Debora's but her friend was too busy to come. So Rachel walked along the path across the farmland as quickly as she could. Some people were already coming back from market or from the farm. They pushed their bicycles through the deep sand, or carried baskets and bowls on their heads.

"What can be wrong with Sara?" Rachel asked herself as she went along. "I do wish Debora was able to come with me."

Sara's compound was quite big. It was very clean. The sandy part was swept and tidy. There were banana, plantain and paw-paw growing along the fence. The fence itself was beginning to fall down. The house was quite big, built of mud bricks with a thatched roof, but it too needed repair. The paint on the doors and window frames had faded under the sun to a greenish grey. The steps up to the verandah were cracked.

Rachel could not see Sara anywhere. None of the small children were around either. She found Mama Sara sitting in the kitchen, beginning to prepare the evening meal. She looked up as Rachel came to the steps.

"Good evening. Has Sara gone out?"

Mama Sara looked at her in a strange way. "No. She's inside the house."

The door was closed. Rachel looked at the door and back at Mama Sara. How strange that someone was inside the house with the door closed at this time of day.

Mama Sara was very busy cutting up vegetables. She did not seem to want to look up. Rachel knew there was something very wrong, but she didn't want to ask what had happened. She went up to the door and knocked.

"Come in."

She pushed open the door. It was dark inside. She could just see Sara sitting on a stool. A tray was on her knees. She was cracking and peeling seeds ready for cooking.

"Who is it?" she asked, turning towards the door.

"It's me!" Rachel said. "It's Rachel. Don't you know me?"

"Oh, Rachel! How nice. Can you find a stool and sit down? I think school started today. How's the new class?"

"Never mind about the class. We're worried about you – Jacob and the other boys, and Debora. Why didn't you come to school?"

"I can never come to school again," Sara said sadly. Her voice sounded dry, as though she had cried until she had no water left in her.

"Sara, what's wrong? What's the matter?" Rachel realised that Sara was not really looking at her. Her eyes were half closed, red and sore. She was looking past Rachel, above her right shoulder.

"I can't see well enough to come to school," she answered in that same dry voice.

Rachel watched Sara's busy fingers searching for seeds on the tray. She did not look down. Her face was turned towards Rachel.

"Do you mean you can't see at all? You're . . ."

"Blind? Not exactly. Sometimes I can see people moving, like shadows. I can see your white blouse and the light from the door. But when the sun is out it hurts my eyes so much. I have to keep them closed. That's all."

Rachel did not know what to say. This was worse than anything she had imagined.

"I'm so sorry, Sara. How did it happen?"

"It started with the headaches I had last term. Then my eyes began to itch and burn. When I went outside, tears began to fall as if I was crying."

"Have you done anything about it? Have you been anywhere to get help?"

Sara sighed. "My mother said some bad thing must be hurting my eyes. She made a wash from herbs, but it didn't help. Then she bought some eyedrops from the man who sells medicines at the market. They cost so much – but they didn't help. I asked her not to buy any more."

"Oh, Sara!"

"The native doctor said I must have gone into a shrine. That's what our neighbours told us. They said I must have seen something forbidden. But I never did anything like that. My uncle . . ." She stopped.

"Yes? Your uncle? What did he say?"

"He said I or my mother must be wicked. God was punishing us."

"Oh no!" Rachel thought of Sara, kind and helpful, and her hardworking mother. "What a cruel thing to say!"

"Yes, I thought so too."

Sara tried to smile, and there was a sad little silence. Rachel didn't know what to say except to repeat that she was very sorry.

"I'm sorry too. And I'm so sad that I can't come to school. Please say hallo to everyone – to Jacob, and Daniel, and Kipi. I expect the new baby is keeping Debora busy. I suppose you're all in the same class again? I'll think of you . . ."

Rachel stayed a little longer. At last she opened the door again. "I have to go home now, Sara. It's time to help with the supper."

Sara felt among the shells for the last few seeds. "Goodbye," she said, and she managed to smile this time.

Rachel said goodnight to Mama Sara. She was still sitting by herself watching the pot on the fire. She hurried home, wanting to cry. She could not remember a time when she had felt so unhappy.

Chapter
| **2** |

Everyone was very upset when Rachel told them the news next day.

"Blind!" said Kipi.

"Nearly blind," Rachel told him.

"It's the same thing. She can't see. Whatever will she do?"

"Whatever can we do, you mean," said Rachel. "We'll have to help her somehow."

"Yes," agreed Jacob.

"Her mother is so upset too," Rachel went on. "She could hardly speak to me. She's usually such a sweet cheerful woman, always busy. But she sat there in the kitchen watching the pot on the fire, saying nothing, doing nothing."

"We could go and visit her," Debora suggested.

"What good will that do?" Kipi objected.

"You'd better stay away from Sara if that's how you feel, Kipi," said Jacob. "Visits are meant to cheer up people in trouble. Visits make them feel better and stronger because other people care about them."

"Visits don't change anything. The problem is still there."

"At least we can go and ask what we can do. Maybe Mama Sara has thought of something by now."

Rachel said, "I've been to that compound often. It's always lively, with children playing and laughing. Mama Sara rushes about, and Sara looks after everything with a book in her hand."

The others nodded. They remembered Sara's compound like that, too.

"Yesterday it was so quiet and empty," Rachel went on. "And everything is getting old and needing repair. Is Mama Sara so poor? I know she's a widow, and there are the children to look after, but is she really so poor?"

No one knew anything about that.

"I suppose Sara could become a beggar," Kipi said as they walked back to class.

"Kipi!" Debora was shocked.

"Shut up if you've nothing better to say," said Rachel angrily.

Everyone was cross. But Jacob knew that many people would agree with Kipi. What could a blind girl do?

That evening Jacob and Daniel went to see Sara. Kipi went with them, but they told him to keep quiet if he had nothing good to say. Debora was still busy with the new baby and Rachel could not manage to come a second time.

"I don't want to come, anyway," she said. "It's too sad."

Mama Sara greeted them as she had greeted Rachel. She looked as though her thoughts were far away.

First the boys went to visit Sara. She came out of the house, pulling a cloth over her eyes. Then she sat down in the darkest corner of the verandah.

"I get so tired of sitting in the house," she said. She started to peel another trayful of seeds. "Today the sun isn't too bright for me."

At first the boys did not know what to say. Sara began to ask them what was happening at school. Soon they were all chatting away happily. Even Kipi joined in. Sara was still Sara, even if she couldn't see properly.

"Let me go and talk to your mother."

Jacob left them and went over to the kitchen. He sat down on a stool. "Mama Sara, how did this happen?"

Jacob was the son of a teacher at the school, so Mama Sara was willing to talk to him about the problem. She told him how the trouble had begun, how it had developed. She told him what she had done, what people had said. She did not say anything about Sara's uncle.

Jacob decided to ask about him. "Isn't there something else that can be done? Is there no one in the family who can help?"

Mama Sara did not answer.

He tried again. "Didn't your husband have a brother? I'm sure Sara once said she had an uncle."

Mama Sara looked angry. "That man! Did Sara know she had an uncle until my kind husband had gone forever? I don't want to talk about him. I'd go to the moon to help Sara, but I wouldn't go to him."

Jacob felt very young and unable to help. He began to speak about something else.

"Sara's trouble came suddenly," he said. "Perhaps it will go again just as suddenly."

Mama Sara looked at him.

"Perhaps Sara will get better one day." He tried to sound hopeful.

"Who can believe that?" said Mama Sara sadly. She began to stir the pot.

After a little while she said, as if to herself, "When Sara was well, she used to do this for me. She used to go to the stream. Now she falls into the water before she can see it."

Jacob made an unhappy sound.

"She used to gather vegetables," Mama Sara went on. "Now she doesn't know if she's picking bitter leaves or sweet herbs. She used to bring home firewood. Now she may put her hand on a snake. She won't know it's there until it's bitten her."

There was a silence.

"The little ones have to go for everything," said Mama Sara sadly. "How much can they bring back?"

Jacob said nothing. What was there to say?

"But these are my problems," she said at last. "What about Sara? What will she do? She sits there like an old grandmother, peeling seeds for the soup. She can't go in the kitchen. Who will marry her?"

Jacob hoped Sara couldn't hear what her mother was saying. He looked quickly across to the verandah. Sara seemed to be listening to Daniel. He could see her face, but it did not tell him anything.

He tried to say something helpful to Mama Sara. Then he got up.

"We must be going now," he said.

"Thank you for your visit," Mama Sara said. Her voice sounded full of sad thoughts.

"Sara . . . We have to go now," Jacob called.

"Yes," said Mama Sara. "Tell her you're going, or she'll never know. She'll still be talking to you when you're halfway home."

Jacob hoped very much that Sara was not listening to her mother.

He was very quiet as they began to walk home. Kipi and Daniel seemed quite happy. Sara had cheered them up.

"She was just the same as always," said Daniel. "I expect she'll get better soon."

Kipi said nothing. He was smiling, but Jacob thought he did not agree with Daniel.

Jacob left the others near their homes, and finished the walk alone. He felt very upset. Mama Sara had shared her trouble with him and he felt as if he was carrying its weight along.

At supper he did not feel like eating much. He tried to swallow what he could. If he did not eat, his mother would start worrying and think he was ill.

After supper he went out to sit on the verandah. It was a beautiful night. The moon shone. The light was almost as bright as daytime, with deep black shadows.

Jacob's father was already sitting there with his small radio. From the other teachers' houses came the sound of voices and laughing. The windows were yellow where the lamps were lit but the moon shone brighter. It hurt Jacob to think of Sara. Her world was dark.

"How was Sara?" his father asked.

Jacob began to tell him the whole story. It was good to speak to someone about it. He felt the load grow lighter as he spoke.

His father listened carefully. "This isn't the end, Jacob," he said at last. "I expect her eyes are painful. She must be upset and afraid . . . her mother too. But her sight needn't be lost for ever. What she needs now is to speak to someone who really knows about eye problems – an eye specialist."

"Perhaps we could buy her some different eye drops," suggested Jacob. "Something better than the kind the medicine seller brings to the market."

His father shook his head. "We'd only be guessing what to do. We could make things worse, not better. We don't know anything about eye problems. An eye specialist would know what's wrong and what to do about it. Sara ought to go to a hospital where the doctors know all about eye problems."

"A specialist hospital."

Jacob's father nodded.

"Mama Sara said she'd go to the moon to help Sara," said Jacob slowly. He looked up at the bright sky.

"She doesn't have to go so far," smiled his father. "She only has to go to Sabah." He thought for a moment. "I suppose for a woman like Mama Sara, Sabah is as hard to reach as the moon."

"You mean she can't afford to take Sara there." Jacob thought of the broken fence and the house which needed repair.

"She wouldn't need a rocket and an astronaut," laughed his father. "But she'd need a great deal of money."

He sighed. "A rich country like America can afford to send men to the moon. Mama Sara can't even afford to buy a train ticket to Sabah."

Jacob nodded. His face was gloomy.

"It's not only a train ticket," went on his father a moment later. "She'd have to pay the doctors at the hospital, buy food, find a place to stay. It's too much for her. And I think she'd be afraid to travel so far, as well."

"It's sad that she doesn't have anyone in her family who can help," said Jacob carefully.

His father seemed to have finished talking about Sara. He picked up his radio and began to listen to the evening news.

Jacob went in to see his mother. He told her about Sara and their visit that afternoon.

His mother shared Mama Sara's thoughts about Sara. "Poor girl. Who will marry her now? She is no use to herself or her family. How sad for her mother!"

"Who is Sara's uncle?" Jacob asked. "Do you know?"

"Does she have an uncle?"

"He's her father's brother."

"Oh, that one. Yes, her father had a brother. I don't think he will ever agree to call himself Sara's uncle."

"Why not?"

"Some old quarrels can last a long time," observed his mother. "You see, Sara's grandfather, the father of her father, had two wives. The two women never liked each other, so I heard."

"What about Sara?" asked Jacob.

"Sara's father was the child of the younger wife. Her uncle is the child of the older wife," explained his mother. "The old man wanted to marry two wives, but he liked the first wife better than the second. There must have been a lot of trouble in that house."

Jacob nodded. He could imagine it.

"Their sons never agreed with each other. Each one took the side of his own mother. They all lived at the coast until the old man died. The elder son took all the property, I heard."

Jacob stared at her in surprise.

"Sara's father came home to this village and built his house here. It all happened years and years ago. Why did you want to know?"

"Sara told me her uncle refused to help. He even said her trouble came because God was punishing her for being wicked."

"Yes," said his mother with a sigh. "He is the kind of man who could say something like that to her. Some people might have that idea, but only a man like her uncle could *say* it to people in trouble. The old quarrel is still alive beween them."

"If her uncle is still at the coast, how could Sara hear from him? Perhaps she wrote to him. That doesn't seem very likely."

"He came back here too, about six years ago."

"But who is he? Do I know him?"

"Of course you do. Everyone knows him. He's the Councillor."

The Councillor! Jacob understood everything now. That was why Mama Sara seemed to have no hope.

Jacob went to bed still thinking hard. He looked out of his bedroom window at the moon. It was almost ready to set now, looking smaller and very far away. But Sabah . . . Sabah was not so far away. Sabah was at the end of the railway line, just two days' slow journey. All that was needed was money.

He made up his mind. He was going to get Sara to Sabah, even if the Councillor himself stood in the way.

Chapter
| 3 |

Jacob called the friends together the next day. His voice was serious. "We've all seen Sara now . . ."

"I haven't," said Debora. "But Rachel has told me everything."

"Well, we can't just say 'how sad' and turn away, can we?" said Jacob. He looked around at the friends. They were all shaking their heads.

"We've got to do something for her," said Rachel.

"But there's nothing to be done," said Kipi. "When someone's blind, that's the end of it."

"No, it isn't." Jacob told them what his father had said. "No one should give up hope until a specialist has looked at the problem."

"When we saw Sara yesterday she seemed quite happy," said Kipi. "She doesn't seem to mind what's happened. She's used to it. You'll only upset her."

"Of course she minds!" said Rachel. "Would you be happy if this had happened to you?"

Kipi looked quite frightened.

"Of course we can't leave her like that if anything can be done," said Daniel. "But Jacob, what can we do to help her?"

"She needs to go to a doctor who knows all about eye problems, a specialist doctor." Jacob took a deep breath. "Papa said that. She ought to go as soon as possible to the eye hospital in Sabah."

"In Sabah!" the others shouted.

"That's a long way," said Daniel. He had travelled more than any of his friends, but he had never been to Sabah.

"It'll cost a lot of money," said Debora. "And when she gets there, does Mama Sara know anyone in the hospital? That's very important. It's hard to get anything done if you don't know anyone to help you."

"The money comes first," said Rachel. "She can't go until she has the money. The other problems don't matter now. When we get the money we can think of what to do about them."

"Did you say 'when' or 'if'?" began Kipi. He stopped when he saw his friends' angry faces.

"How can we get the money?" asked Debora. "If only we knew someone rich."

There was a silence.

There were no rich people living in the village. Some people had built big houses nearby, but they did not live in them. They were working in the cities, making money. They had built the houses so that they could come home to live in the village when they were old and tired of working far away.

"I've seen reports in the newspaper about people who are ill," Daniel told them. "They ask the readers of the newspaper to send money to help them. Then the people can go to a hospital in England or America. It costs a lot of money to do that," he added.

"Yes." Rachel nodded. "When I was staying with my Auntie, I saw a picture in the newspaper of a little boy. He was very weak and small. They said he had something wrong with his heart. He needed to go to a special hospital in America for an operation on his heart."

"To America!" said Daniel.

"The newspaper kept asking people to send money. They needed thousands and thousands. People sent enough money in the end, but it took about six months. He could have died while he was waiting for the money."

"That was a big problem," said Jacob. "This is really only a little problem. It just seems big to us because Sara is our friend. People wouldn't think it was important enough."

"We don't need thousands and thousands," said Debora. "It only seems a lot of money because we don't have any at all."

The others were still working out the cost of going to Sabah.

"Train fare to get Sara there and back again . . ."

"And don't forget she has to get from here to the railway station. That's a long way."

"She has to buy food while she's there."

"She needs somewhere to stay."

Daniel suggested an amount of money.

"You'll have to double that," said Jacob. "Someone has to go with Sara. She can't go by herself."

"It's all too much, isn't it?" said Kipi. He looked at their faces to see if they were angry. Then he went on. "There are too many problems."

"We said we'd take one problem at a time," Jacob reminded him.

"The first one is to get some money!" said Daniel and Debora.

"Right. Without money, nothing can happen. How can we get some money?"

"Earn it?" suggested Daniel. "But how? There's not much paid work for us here. We help our parents. There's no money. People either have just enough, or they're poor."

"That reminds me," said Rachel. "Why is Mama Sara so poor? She farms a big piece of land along the river. That's good land."

"That was years ago. I'm sure she hasn't farmed that land for a long time," said Daniel. "I've seen labourers working that land when I pass on my way to our farm. I don't think Mama Sara could afford to pay labourers."

"She may have sold it," said Kipi.

"But then why not use the money to help Sara?"

"You can see she doesn't have any money." Jacob remembered the unhappy woman sitting by her fire. "All of their clothes are old and worn. The children look hungry. Mama Sara wouldn't hide away her money and not look after her family. What has happened?"

Debora agreed. "It can't be that she's used the money badly. If we were talking about a man, we'd guess he was gambling and drinking. But Mama Sara is a very good woman."

"Perhaps she used all the money when her husband was ill. Then he died."

"That could be. Next time I pass that way I'll ask the labourers who they work for," promised Daniel.

"Let's get back to raising the money," said Jacob. "That's the important thing at the moment. Does anyone have any idea how we could raise some money?"

"I have," said Debora.

The others looked at her hopefully.

"Do you remember when the women's meeting learned a new dance? They invited everyone to come and watch. They collected money."

"We can't dance," objected Kipi.

"I know we can't dance! What else can we do so that people will come and watch us?"

"Who – just the five of us? Nothing." Kipi thought the whole idea was stupid.

"What about a play?" suggested Rachel. "You remember the play they put on here when we were still in Primary School? We all came to see it."

"I remember," said Debora. "It was very good, but rather sad."

"That was the whole school," said Kipi. "And those days were different, anyway. Things are hard now, and there are only five of us."

17

"I think that's a good idea, Rachel." Jacob ignored Kipi. "If we can find a good play, I think we should try to put it on."

"Will we sell tickets?" asked Debora, leaping all the problems in between and thinking only of the end.

"We can decide later. We'd have to print tickets or make them in some way. We could just collect some money, like the women's meeting did."

"Some people won't pay," Kipi told him.

"They will if we tell them what the money's for," said Daniel. "Everyone will give something. No one could refuse."

"Then that's decided," said Jacob. "First, we agree to raise some money and send Sara to hospital. Second, we agree to look around for plays. Third – is there a third?"

"Yes," said Daniel. "We agree to make up our minds to do our best and succeed." He looked hard at Kipi.

"Agreed!" said everyone.

Kipi said it less loudly than everyone else. But he said it all the same.

Jacob went home and searched his father's bookcase. His father kept all his books very carefully, even the books from his own school days. Jacob felt sure he would find what he wanted there.

He found several plays which had been set books for English Literature exams in past years. He took these down and sat down to read them.

Jacob soon found that most of them were long, all were difficult and none were suitable for what the friends wanted to do. He knew there would be many problems in putting on a play. He had not begun to think about those yet. A play had to be found first, and these plays were no use at all.

The school no longer had a library. But he knew that there were books in a cupboard in the staff room.

"Do you think there are any plays in that cupboard?" he asked his father.

"There may be. It's possible. Why do you want to read plays?"

So Jacob had to explain. His father wanted to encourage his son, so he said: "That's a very kind idea. It's something that should be done."

He thought for a moment. "It's going to be difficult . . . I'm sure you know that already . . . but go ahead. If you think I can help you or advise you, call on me."

"Thank you, Papa," said Jacob.

"For a start, come to the staff room with me on Saturday morning. Take a look in that cupboard by the door. There might be something suitable there if you're lucky."

There were several teachers in the staff room when they went in. Jacob greeted them politely. He waited while his father explained what he wanted.

"No problem," they said. "But why do you want to read plays?"

Jacob had to explain again.

"Kind thought," said Mr Buah. "Go ahead. See if you can find anything."

Jacob found several more books of plays. He asked if he could take them home so that he could look at them properly. He made a list of the book titles, signed it with the date, and gave it to his father.

After he had gone away, the teachers looked at each other. Then they looked at Jacob's father.

"It's a kind thought," said Mr Buah again. "I hope it doesn't get him into trouble with you-know-who!"

Jacob's mother was also worried about this. She spoke her fears openly to her husband when he came home.

"Do you think the Councillor will be angry?"

She was watching Jacob. He was carefully cleaning the dusty books on the verandah.

"Why should he be angry?"

"He doesn't like Sara's family. Perhaps he won't want anyone to try to help them."

"I hope the efforts of a few young people in school won't really matter to him," said her husband. "He should have more important things to think about. He's supposed to be looking after the people of five villages."

"Yes," she said. She did not sound at all sure about it. "He's powerful, you know."

"Jacob and his friends want to help Sara. I'm not going to refuse to help them because the Councillor may not like it. The Councillor may want to carry on a quarrel that should have ended many years ago. That doesn't concern Jacob."

"Of course it doesn't," she agreed quickly.

"Our children are giving all of us a lesson," he added.

The Councilor may not want to be given a lesson, thought Jacob's mother. But she kept quiet.

Chapter 4

The friends soon found it was not easy to choose a suitable play. When they met, most of them were carrying the same English Literature set books.

"I know people won't like these," said Debora. "They're all too long and difficult."

"They might like Macbeth," said Daniel. "All that fighting!"

"What about us?" Rachel reminded him. "All that learning! The play would go on for hours. People would get tired of watching it."

"Don't forget the clothes for the play," Rachel said. "We couldn't find the right clothes for Macbeth and plays like that, set long ago or in other countries."

"So the play has to be about here and now," said Debora. "In this country, today."

"That's right. We'll have to wear our everyday clothes, or perhaps traditional dress. We can borrow those if we need them."

"There are too many characters in these plays," said Debora. "That's another problem. Do you think we ought to bring in more people?"

Jacob thought about that. Then he said, "No, I don't. If we are too many, we'll need a teacher or two to help keep order and make people come to practise."

"That's right." Debora sat down to make a list. "We need a play with only five characters, two girls, three boys."

"This is our own project," added Jacob. "We're ready to work at it. Others might not be ready to work so hard."

The friends found that it was not at all easy to find a play like that. Some had too many characters in them, or they were for all girls, or all boys. Some of the short easy plays had the right number of parts but were too well known. The others groaned when Debora read out the titles. Everyone had read them in Class 1 or 2, not just once, but many times.

"Boring!" they agreed. "No one will want to come and listen to these old plays again."

Another week passed. They still had not found a suitable play. Jacob decided that they were wasting too much time.

"There's only one thing we can do," he said. "If we can't find the right play ready-made for us, then we must make our own."

"Yes," agreed Rachel. "And I know where we can get one. Why don't we use that story Sara made up? She read it to us, changing her voice to fit the people in the story. We said then it was like a play."

"I remember," said Debora. "The Chief has a very quiet wife and daughter and he boasts about how well he rules his family."

"Oh, yes! But then he wants his daughter to marry a big politician, and his son to marry the daughter of a rich businessman."

"That's right. And she wants to marry the politician but . . ."

For the next ten minutes they told each other the best bits of the story and laughed a lot.

"That's a great idea," Jacob said. "I'm sure you've found the answer to the problem. Sara's story will do very well. It's very funny. It's new so that people won't know what's going to happen next. They'll want to know what the end will be."

"And we can use traditional dress and everyday clothes," said Rachel.

"But remember," Jacob went on, "Sara wrote this as a story. She'll have to write it again as a play. The words the characters say to each other must tell the whole story. She'll have to do that before we can begin."

"You mean," said Kipi, catching up at last, "Sara will write the play? But plays come in books."

"Someone had to write them before they could become books."

"Not someone like Sara."

"Why not? Sara's going to write this one. One day perhaps it will be a book."

"She can't see to write anything," Kipi argued.

"No problem. She can think it out and tell us. One of us can write it down for her."

Kipi was still finding problems. "There would be three parts for girls and four for boys. Don't forget the Chief's wife and son."

"Those are just little parts," said Debora. "Perhaps we can get two people for those parts."

"I thought you said you didn't want to bring in other people."

"Not *lots* of other people," Jacob explained patiently.

The others groaned.

"Kipi, stop making things difficult," said Rachel.

"She'll want to know why," said Daniel suddenly. "Mama Sara will want to know what we're doing. We'll have to go to Sara's house every day until the play is written down."

"Of course we'll tell them what we're doing," Jacob said. "Mama Sara said she'd go to the moon to help Sara. She won't try to stop us from helping her."

"But if you tell them," Kipi pointed out, "Sara will know all about what you're trying to do."

"Well of course she will," Daniel shouted. "That's what we just said. What's wrong with that?"

"I thought we were keeping it a secret," said Kipi. "When we have enough money, we'll go and give it to her. *If* we get enough," he added.

Rachel opened her mouth to shout at him, but he hurried on.

"And if we don't get the money she won't be disappointed . . . because she won't know about it. Do you see?"

"Yes, I see," said Jacob slowly. "But it won't be possible to keep our play a secret. When we start practising, people will get to know what we're doing. I'm sure quite a lot of people already know. I had to tell some teachers why I wanted those books of plays. My father and mother know all about it."

"So do mine," said Rachel.

"And mine," added Debora.

"But won't Mama Sara be disappointed if we say we're going to help Sara and then we don't raise the money?"

"Kipi," said Rachel, "Start from this moment to believe that we *are* going to raise the money. If you try hard enough, you'll be able to believe that."

"I think Mama Sara will feel better when she knows we're trying to do something to help her," said Jacob. There was something in his voice that stopped them from arguing.

Next day they went to Sara's house and explained that they wanted to help.

Mama Sara sighed. "I don't think you can help us. I don't think anyone can help us. But thank you, my children!"

"Don't give up hope," begged Jacob. "My father says Sara must go to the eye hospital in Sabah. The doctors know everything about eye problems. Perhaps they can help Sara."

"Sabah!" she shouted, angrily. "How far is that? Can I go there and come back in one day? Who will lock up the chickens and cut grass for the goat? Who will take care of the children? How much

will it all cost? Go to Sabah! I think all of you must want to make fun of me."

"No, no, of course not," said Rachel quickly. "We're very serious about this. Sara's our friend and we want to help her. If we can get the money to pay for the journey, will you take her to Sabah?"

"If you get the money! How will you do that? I hope you won't steal it. Will you find it in the bush?"

"That's our problem," said Jacob. "We won't steal, I promise. But if we can get the money, will you agree to go to Sabah?"

"Of course I'll go. You bring me the money and I'll go to the moon. I told you before. I could sell the goat."

"No, don't sell anything. Leave this to us. Let me explain. This is what we plan to do."

Mama Sara listened silently while Jacob explained. Then she looked at each of them in turn.

"Good children! Good, good children! Can Sara make up a play for you? Will people pay money to see it? And where will they come to see it?"

"She can do it," said Rachel.

"Leave the rest to us," said Jacob.

Perhaps Mama Sara thought he knew the answers to all her questions. He hoped so.

"All right," she said at last. "You're good children."

She did not sound very sure about their idea, but at least she did not refuse.

The friends went to talk to Sara.

"Oh, how kind of you to think of doing this," she said, smiling towards them. "Which play will you put on?"

"Your play," explained Jacob again.

Sara was surprised for a moment. Then she began to rearrange the story in her quick mind. "I can improve it this time."

Jacob thought how clever she was. He knew Sara was clever in class but this was something new.

"When can we come and write down the words?" asked Debora.

"Let's start tomorrow. I won't be able to do it all at once. I won't get it right the first time. There'll have to be changes. Do you have lots of paper?"

"I'll bring a pile of old election notices," said Debora. "Mama was saving them to wrap up groundnuts, but there are hundreds of them."

"There's one problem," said Sara, already deep in the story. "You only have two girls. There are three in the story."

She thought for a few mintues. "I know," she said. "The wife won't say much. Just 'Yes, my lord, no, my lord', very quietly. She can keep her face covered by a shawl. Then the same person can play the chief's wife *and* the rich businessman's daughter."

"Do you think it will work?" Kipi spoke up at last. "And what about the Chief's son . . . four boys' parts and three of us."

"I'll think of something," said Sara. She was still working out how to arrange the girls' parts. "I must make sure the two characters aren't on stage at the same time."

"And the girl who plays both parts needs time to change her dress," said Rachel.

Kipi opened his mouth to say something but Jacob made signs to him to shut up.

"Talking of being on stage," said Sara. "Where will you act this play? There's nowhere in school since the assembly hall was burned down last year."

"Let's get the play written first," said Jacob.

He wished people would stop asking him this question. He had no idea of the answer.

"You think out the play during the day," he went on. "One of us will come over after school. Whoever comes will sit with you and write down everything you've made up."

"That's fine. Make sure you don't give Debora or Rachel all the hard work." Sara sounded like her old self again.

"We promise."

"Bring plenty of paper. Act one, scene one. Just like Shakespeare," said Sara, and she laughed.

Chapter 5

The friends now became very busy indeed. One or other of them went to Sara's house every evening. They had to write down the words Sara had thought of during the day. They also read some of the pages written earlier so that she could make changes.

This needed a lot of arranging. The friends had to explain to their mothers what was so important every afternoon. Mama Sara's neighbours noticed what was happening and asked what was going on. She told them all about it.

"That's called good publicity," said Jacob. "People will find out about the play and why we're putting it on. Then when we're ready they'll come to see what we've been doing."

At last Sara felt satisfied with her work. Each of the friends had to make a copy of the play to study. As they made their copies, they found that they were beginning to learn the words.

Jacob said that they must go and read the whole play to Sara, taking their own parts, in case she wanted to make any more changes.

That was fun. The young children sat listening and laughing. Even Mama Sara left her kitchen to come and watch.

"Sara wrote that?" she asked at the end. She was still wiping the tears of laughter from her eyes.

"You know she did!"

"It's wonderful."

Sara looked very pleased. She suggested a few changes. Everyone wrote them on their own copy of the play.

"And now," said Jacob, "All we have to do is to go and finish learning the words."

But of course that was not all they had to do.

Their parents all thought the play project was a kind thought, even if they did not really believe it would ever happen. They allowed the friends time to practise when they should be working at home. But (and it was a big "but") they all said they must be careful to keep up with their school work.

Everyone had to learn their words while they did other jobs.

Soon they found that they knew their own parts and most of what the others had to say too. They could even remind each other when anyone forgot what came next.

As if that wasn't enough to keep them busy, Jacob decided that one of them should visit Sara at least twice a week. He did not want her to feel lonely now that the excitement of writing the play was over.

He was still very puzzled about how poor the family was.

"Why didn't Sara know that the Councillor was her uncle until her father had died?" he asked Daniel.

"Is he her uncle? I didn't know that. Perhaps he came to the funeral."

"My mother says the two brothers never liked each other."

"He could still feel sorry afterwards and come to the funeral."

"He couldn't have felt sorry for very long. He refused to help Sara when this trouble began. She told me. He was unkind to her."

Two days later Daniel came to Jacob with some news.

"Guess who owns that land by the river? The Councillor!"

"No!"

"I saw some men working there so I stopped and asked them. They said the land belonged to the Councillor."

Jacob stared.

Now that everyone had learned their words, the friends began to practise the play properly. Jacob asked his father if they could use a classroom when school was over. They imagined a stage at one end of the classroom, instead of rows of desks.

"Where are we going to act this play?" Debora asked. "Could we do it here in school?"

"Where in school could we do it?" Jacob said. "We need to have three levels, somewhere high so that everyone can see, two steps and a flat space for the dancers."

"Dancers?" asked Rachel.

"Didn't I tell you?" said Debora. "The little girls from the Primary School will dance for the Chief in the play, when he is sitting with his guests."

There were nods and cries of "Good! Good!"

"There are some big tables in the store-room," said Daniel. "Do you think we could make a stage?"

They went to look. The tables were high but they did not look very safe. Several had legs that were loose and shaky. Others were broken.

"I don't think these will do." Rachel shook her head. "They aren't safe to stand on, even if the Principal allowed us to use them."

"There aren't enough of them, anyway," said Debora. The baby was asleep on her back. She often brought him to practices. "Only six. The stage needs to be bigger than that."

"What about using the wooden benches?" Daniel suggested.

There were more of these, and they were very heavy. But some were long and some were short, and all seemed to be of different heights.

"These won't do either," said Kipi. "Someone could trip and fall off."

"I didn't think we could put the play on here at school," said Jacob.

He led the way out of the store-room. "I was thinking of the Church Hall. That has a raised part at one end which we could use as a stage. There are chairs there, too, for people to sit on."

"If anyone comes to see us," said Kipi.

"Shut up!" they all told him.

"We need to take a look, then ask for permission to use it. Do we have to ask the Caretaker or the Pastor? Who knows the Caretaker best?"

"My brother knows him well," said Kipi. "I'll ask him to find out."

Jacob wished that someone else but Kipi was going to talk to the Caretaker. Kipi still did not believe that anything was going to work out right.

When the others had gone, Jacob borrowed a bicycle and went to see Sara. He wanted to ask if she had any ideas about where they could show the play if they could not use the Church Hall.

Just as he was about to leave Sara's compound, he suddenly remembered about the land by the river.

He turned back to Sara. "Doesn't your mother own some land by the river? I wanted to ask her, but she's gone to see the neighbours."

"Oh, please don't ask her. She doesn't like to talk about it. She saved money from her trading. She gave it to my father to buy that land. It's very good land. She grew tomatoes, pepper, maize and vegetables there. She was doing well."

"What went wrong?"

"When Papa died, his brother . . . you know who I mean – the Councillor – came and said the land belonged to him. Everything that belonged to his brother now belonged to him. He took the land. He refused even to let Mama harvest the crops she'd planted."

"How mean! Didn't she complain to anyone?"

"Who can she complain to? To the Chief? The Councillor is very close to him. He seems to have more money than the Chief. The Councillor talks to the people from the government. The Chief doesn't want to annoy him."

"How do you know?" asked Jacob slowly.

"It's what we guessed. The Chief agreed to look into it, when we asked him. But nothing ever happened. Mama asked him again, later. But he said he hadn't had a chance to do anything. Then he started getting angry. So she stopped worrying him about it."

"If everything that belonged to your Papa now belongs to the Councillor, surely he should look after you."

"Hum!" said Sara. "He doesn't see things that way."

Jacob was angry. "Why did people choose him to be their Councillor? He's a horrible man."

Sara shook her head. "He can talk well. He sounds important. He wanted to be Councillor. Most people, except the old men, don't have the time. The old men don't want to go to district meetings. They like family and village meetings better, where they know everything."

"What a horrible man!" said Jacob again.

He said goodbye to Sara and rode home. His mother met him at the gate before he could reach the house.

"Jacob, what have you been doing? The Councillor is here. He's come to complain about you to your father. He sounds very angry."

"I haven't done anything wrong," said Jacob. "Are you sure he's angry?"

The Councillor must have heard about the play, he thought. *Surely he hasn't come to complain about that? Perhaps after all he's planning to help Sara himself.*

"Don't worry," he told his mother, and went up to the house.

The Councillor was a large, soft-looking man with a light, oily skin. He looked as if he ate very well but didn't do much work. Jacob's father looked strong and hard beside him.

"Jacob, the Councillor is complaining about you," Jacob's father said. But he did not sound angry.

"Yes, Papa?"

Jacob stood up straight and tall like a soldier.

"Would you like to say again why you are complaining?" the teacher asked very politely.

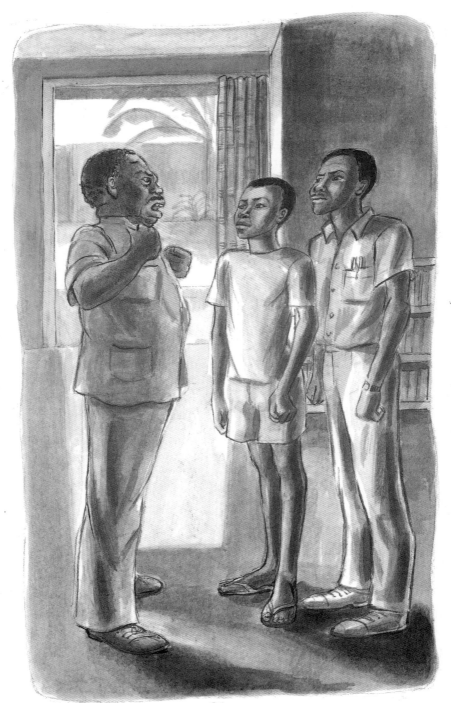

"Your son is trying to spoil my family name!"

"How is that possible, Councillor?" asked Jacob's father. "Everyone knows what you are."

"He's trying to make people believe I'm failing in my duty to the family."

"Are you doing anything like that, Jacob?"

"No, Papa."

"He's going about begging for money, pretending he's going to give sight to a blind girl."

"Are you begging for money, Jacob?"

"No, Papa."

"Is this blind person one of your family, Councillor?"

Jacob looked down and tried not to smile. If the Councillor said "No", he had no cause to complain. If he said "Yes" then his father could ask why the Councillor did not do something for her himself.

The Councillor pretended not to hear.

"You'd better control your son, teacher. Or you could be moved to a place even worse than this."

"I'm sure the people will be glad to hear what you think of their village . . . and their votes," said his father in a cold voice.

Jacob stared at him in surprise. He had never heard his father, a man of peace, speak like that before.

The Councillor got up and went away without a word.

"Papa, I'm sorry if I'm making trouble for you. Could he make you lose your job?"

"I don't think so. He could get me moved away from this school. What if he did? There will be students to teach wherever I go. It would be much worse to give way to a bully."

He smiled at his son. "Don't worry about me, Jacob. Just remember the Councillor is now an angry and dangerous man. So be careful. Go ahead with what you're planning to do, but be ready for trouble."

Chapter
6

The Councillor's visit made the whole project seem different. Jacob's father did not seem to worry about it at all. But his mother was full of questions.

"What did you do, Jacob? The Councillor's never come here before. He looked so angry."

"Tell her, Jacob," his father said.

"The Councillor doesn't like it because I'm trying to help Sara. I'm the one who started the plan to raise some money for her, so that she could go to the hospital. He came to tell me to stop."

"Is that so? Does he want to help her?"

"No, Mama."

His mother shook her head. "It's a bad thing to keep an old quarrel alive for so long. The brothers didn't like each other. Now the Councillor hates the widow and her children. It's a very bad thing."

Jacob thought about telling his mother that the Councillor could move his father to another school. But he decided to leave that to his father. He could tell her himself if he wanted.

"Will you stop practising the play?" his mother wanted to know.

"No, not unless Papa tells me to stop."

"Quite right," she said, surprising him. "Next year that man will be asking people to vote for him again. To try to stop you helping your sick friend . . . No, that wouldn't be a good story for people to hear. He likes being the Councillor."

Her husband agreed. "I don't think he will do anything to stop you in a way that people can see. Just look out for trouble that people *can't* see, that's all, Jacob."

Jacob wondered if he should tell his friends about the Councillor's visit . . . and what he had said. Perhaps they would want to stop. That would be too bad. They had all done so much work. Sara and her mother were looking happier, too.

But was it fair not to tell the others? The Councillor was an important person. Could he do anything to the friends – or to their parents? Jacob thought he could not. The only person who worked for the government was Jacob's own father.

He was still thinking about this as he got ready for that evening's practice. In fact, he had almost decided to tell the friends about the Councillor when his father spoke to him.

"Jacob, I want to bring someone to watch you practising. I hope you won't mind."

"Of course not, Papa." Jacob was very curious.

"Yes, he's a friend of mine. He came down from Sabah to see his married sister. And you could use some good publicity."

Jacob waited for more, but his father did not explain what he meant.

When Jacob arrived at the school, the others were already waiting. "Someone's coming to watch us," he told them. "He's Papa's friend."

"Oh no! We're not ready yet for anyone to watch us," Kipi said. He looked worried.

"Why not?" asked Rachel. "They know we're still practising. Perhaps they'll advise us and tell us how to do things better."

"Here they come!" called Daniel.

The friends greeted Jacob's father and his friend from Sabah.

"Carry on with your practice. Forget about us," said Jacob's father. "Imagine that we are not here."

It was difficult to do that, but Jacob stepped forward to begin the practice.

"You know I am the Chief of this town," he began, "And more than the Chief of this family." He said the words as though he was very proud of himself. But he was wearing everyday clothes and holding a stick instead of a staff of office.

The two men listened and smiled, and laughed in all the right places. Everyone played their part well, and nobody forgot their words.

"Well done!" Jacob's father and the stranger clapped loudly at the end.

"Do you write plays too?" Kipi asked.

"No," said the stranger. "But I watch quite a lot of politicians."

He brought out a small camera. It had a lot of switches and knobs on it.

"I'd like to take a few photos. Do you mind?"

"We aren't dressed up," Rachel said.

"That doesn't matter. Let's have that part where the Chief is trying to persuade the politician . . . That's right. Now the part where the daughter is explaining to her mother why she won't marry the man . . ."

He took about ten photos of different scenes. Then he said goodbye and left with Jacob's father, both of them smiling.

"What do you think?" Jacob's father asked as they walked along.

"Congratulations. Young Jacob is a worthy son of his father. Nice young people."

"Do you think they'll succeed in this?"

"Why not? They're trying hard, and they deserve to succeed. Do you know this girl they want to help?"

"Yes, I do," said Jacob's father. "Poor little Sara. She wrote the story, you know. She's changed it a lot to make a better play. She's a very clever girl. She could do great things in life if she gets the chance."

"I'm interested in this. Can you help me to interview Sara? When I leave on Tuesday, we must keep in touch. I want to know what happens, everything. There's a story for me in this, I'm sure of it."

The friends were still talking in the classroom.

"You see," Debora said when their guests had gone, "People are going to laugh. They're supposed to laugh. That means we have to stop talking while they're laughing. If we don't, they're going to miss the next part of the story."

"Or we could say those lines again when they're quiet," said Rachel.

"Any other ideas?" Jacob asked. "Kipi, is there any news of the Church Hall?"

"Yes. My brother and I saw the Caretaker. He said we could

come any time. We can collect the key from his house."

"Why don't we all go now and have a look at it?" suggested Daniel.

The Church Hall stood near the Mission compound, by itself in a sandy space with a wall round it. Kipi unlocked the gate and they went in.

There was quite a big room, half-full of heavy wooden benches and battered metal chairs. The dusty floor was made of cement.

At one end there was a raised area, two cement blocks higher than the floor. It was rather narrow and there was a wooden reading desk in the middle of it.

"There isn't much space," said Daniel. "I hope we can move that desk. I know Sara is clever at writing, but even she'll find it difficult to have a reading desk in the middle of all the action!"

Jacob went to the desk and pushed. It shook a little.

"We can move it when we have to. Let's leave it there now."

Everyone was looking around. There certainly was not much space.

"We'll have to put the chairs at least six feet away from the stage. Then we can use some of the floor, for the dancers."

There were two small rooms, one on each side of the stage, where the actors could wait their turn to come out. There were no curtains.

Rachel pointed to the two small rooms. "That's good," she said. "The politician can go out on the left side. He can run round the end of hall and come in again from the right side – where the Chief isn't expecting him to be."

"Let's hope it isn't raining," said Kipi.

Nobody took any notice of him.

"It's rather a dirty place, isn't it?" Daniel was looking at the walls. "It must be years since it was painted."

"People clean it up when they're going to have a wedding, or something like that. No one ever paints it. We'll clean it up too."

"It'll be fine," Rachel sounded eager. "You'll see."

"Er . . . before we go," Jacob began. "I want to tell you something."

As quickly as he could, he described the Councillor's visit. He tried not to make too much or too little of what had happened.

"He doesn't like Sara or her mother," he explained. "That's why he doesn't want us to help them. Sara said he took her mother's land."

"Yes," Debora agreed. "I think that's true. I heard my mother talking about it. The Councillor said it belonged to him, so his brother had only borrowed it."

"The two brothers weren't friendly. I don't believe the Councillor lent Sara's father anything, even a leaky bucket. And this was very good land."

"He even refused to let them take the crops that were ready. My mother met the children coming back that morning, I remember. The young ones were crying. She asked what was wrong and they told her. That Councillor is horrible."

"He's very rich, too," Daniel told them. "He has a motor bike. Why did he take the land that didn't belong to him? He has enough already."

"He's very important," Kipi reminded them. "If he doesn't want us to help Sara, he'll find some way of stopping us."

Nobody believed him. "How will he do that?" asked Rachel.

Kipi shook his head.

"He won't be able to stop us," said Debora.

"That's that, then," said Jacob. He was glad he had told them the truth. "Next practice is on Wednesday, here at the Hall."

They locked the door behind them, and walked out of the compound.

"We'll have to decide soon when we're going to put on the play," said Jacob. "We'll have to tell everyone about it as soon as we've fixed a date. How shall we do that? We want everyone to come to see it."

They all felt they had made a big step nearer success. Practising in the Hall instead of in the classroom made the play seem more real.

On Wednesday Jacob was waiting at the Hall gate before Kipi arrived with the key.

"What's wrong, Jacob?"

"Nothing's wrong."

"You look as if you've had some news."

"I have . . . good news. Let's wait for the others."

One by one they came in, Debora with the baby as usual.

"Listen," Jacob began. "I've had a letter from the man who watched us act at school . . . the man who took the photos. Do you remember?"

They nodded. They wondered why he looked so excited and pleased. What could this good news be?

"Listen. This is what it says." He took the letter out of his pocket and began to read.

"Dear Jacob, Your father may have told you that I am a newspaper journalist. I work on the News of the Nation *in Sabah."*

"Did he tell you?" asked Debora.

"No. I thought he was just a friend. He goes on:

"When I came back from your village, I made some enquiries at the eye hospital. A team of doctors are to visit in two months' time. They'll stay for three months. All the treatment will be free, even operations."

"Free!" they all shouted.

"Please do your best to send Sara here to meet these doctors."

"There," said Jacob, folding the letter. "What do you say to that?"

"Let's fix the dates for the play," said Rachel.

Chapter 7

The good news about free treatment at the eye hospital made the friends work even harder. They practised every morning in the Church Hall. Sara changed some scenes in the play to give actors time to get round the end of the Hall without being out of breath.

They began to borrow everything they would need to use. They fixed the date of the first performance of the play. There would be four performances, starting on the fifteenth of the next month.

"When shall we collect the money?" Rachel asked.

"If we wait for the end and then ask for money, some people will say it was no good and go away," said Kipi. "If we sell tickets first, people won't buy them for the first performance. They'll wait to hear if it's any good. Then they'll decide if it's worth paying to come and see it."

"And how will we keep away people who stay outside?" asked Daniel. "They'll climb up to watch through the windows."

"Let's take a collection halfway through," suggested Debora. "After the little girls have danced for the Chief and his guests. Everyone will want to know what happens next."

So that was agreed.

More and more people asked when they were going to see the play. So nobody was surprised when the Caretaker came in one evening.

Kipi was busy fastening pieces of black and white goatskin around the handles of two machetes. Then he began to tie red string around them to make them look fine.

The Caretaker frowned. "Why are those machetes in here?"

"We use them in the play," Kipi explained.

"Are you cutting firewood in this play?"

"No . . . Two of the big men want to fight and so . . ."

"A fight? In the Church Hall?"

"Not a real fight! It's just a play, you know."

He tied the string and waved the machete in the air. It looked fine. Kipi was pleased.

He looked at the Caretaker, but the man was still frowning.

"I'm going to stay and watch," he said firmly.

"No problem. We often have guests at our practices," said Kipi grandly.

The others had come in while Kipi was talking to the Caretaker. Now he turned to them and explained that the Caretaker wished to stay and watch. The practice began.

The actors had improved greatly since Jacob's father and his journalist friend had watched them in the classroom. Now they were on a stage. They even had some scenery – a bench and a big chair for the Chief's house, a basket and a pot for his wife's kitchen.

The Caretaker sat and watched. He was sitting in the empty space at their end of the hall. He did not speak. He did not laugh. The actors almost forgot about him as the practice went on. They were all happy when they stood in line and made their bows to him.

"Very good!" said Jacob. "We're nearly there."

The Caretaker got up. "I can't allow it," he said.

The friends were so surprised that nobody knew what to say. They stood and stared at him. Then everyone spoke at once.

"What do you mean?"

"Why do you say that?"

"Why can't you allow it?"

"There's nothing wrong with it!"

"It's a very good play," said Jacob. "We've worked hard at it."

"The daughter of the Chief won't obey her father," said the Caretaker sternly. "Isn't that what happens? It isn't right to teach children not to obey their parents. I can't allow you to teach this in the Church Hall."

"But, Sir!" Jacob could not believe what he was hearing. "We're not teaching that. We're . . ."

The Caretaker did not want to listen. "The Church Hall is for, well, serious things. Important meetings and . . . and so on."

"Weddings?" Kipi looked very angry. Everyone knew noisy wedding parties, with loud music, eating and drinking, were held in the hall.

"Weddings are serious. The Church Hall is not the place where children should play."

"But we're not playing," Kipi pointed out. "I told you what we were going to do when I came with my brother to ask you if we could use the Hall. I explained everything. We're *acting* a play."

He was so angry he had to take a deep breath before he spoke again.

"I told you why we are doing this, too. I even told you the story. You knew everything about it, and you said we could use the Hall. Why have you changed your mind?"

The Caretaker did not want to look at their disappointed faces. He felt sorry for what he had done.

"I can ask about it at the next Committee meeting," he said.

"When does the Committee meet next?" asked Jacob.

He had guessed who was behind this. What had his father said? Expect trouble!

"In three months' time."

Three months! The friends tried hard to persuade the Caretaker to change his mind. But he refused.

Sadly they picked up the pot and the basket and went out.

At first they were all angry and disappointed. They blamed the Caretaker for being so unkind. But then they began to think about a new way to put on the play.

"What shall we do?" said Daniel to Jacob.

"Is there anywhere else we can use?" asked Debora.

"There's the Community Hall, I suppose," said Jacob.

Nobody looked any happier. The Community Hall was only used at election time, or when some very important person was visiting the village. That did not happen very often. For the rest of the time it stood locked and empty on the edge of the next village.

"Could we get permission to use the Community Hall?" Kipi wondered. His eyes were still red with anger.

"Let's go and look at it," Jacob said. "It may be all right."

The Manager of the Community Hall was surprised to see five sad-faced young people walking up to his house. They were carrying a basket and an empty pot.

"How are your parents?" he asked Jacob. He knew Jacob's father well. "I hope they're fine."

Jacob answered him. Then he asked about the health of the Manager's family.

"They are fine," said the Manager. "Now, can I help you in some way?"

"Please may we look inside the Community Hall?" asked Jacob.

"Yes, you may . . . but why?"

So Jacob explained.

"It's a big place," said the Manager. He rubbed his chin with a rough finger. He knew Jacob's father was a responsible person. He did not want to tell these young people to go away. But still . . .

"Perhaps you'd better take a look," he said at last. "Have you ever been here before? No. I think you'll have a surprise."

He went inside the house and came out with a bunch of keys. "Here you are. Bring back the keys when you go."

He watched them walking away. "A play? Here?" he said to himself. "I don't think so."

"Goodness, this place is *big*!" Jacob always hoped for the best, but even he felt worried by the size of the Community Hall.

It seemed to be built for giants, not people. The raised part for the stage was more than a metre high. Everywhere was painted dark green, and it smelled of dust. The huge floor space was empty.

"How many people will come to see us?" asked Debora.

"This place will swallow them up," said Kipi. "Everyone will laugh at us."

"Kipi, we have to try," said Rachel. "Think of Sara!"

"Let's practise a bit in here," said Jacob. He hoped this would help them to get over their surprise and worry.

The huge hall swallowed their voices and made them sound like bats squeaking.

"It won't do," said Jacob.

"Isn't there anywhere else?" asked Rachel. She sounded worried. "We must try. We said we'd act the play on the fifteenth. We could wait, I suppose. But then what about those doctors at Sabah? Everyone will rush for the free treatment."

They came out and Jacob locked the door. He went to return the keys. "How do we get permission to use the Hall?"

The Manager rubbed his chin again. "You write to me . . . or maybe your father should write. Say when and why you want to use it. Then I'll ask the Secretary to the Council to agree. Usually it only takes a few days."

"Thank you."

Jacob went back to the others and told them what the Manager had said.

"Will your father write for us?"

"Of course he will."

"But the Councillor will make sure we don't get permission," said Kipi.

"I'm afraid so. But my father will still try."

Jacob's father wrote to the Manager. But in six days an answer came. It refused them permission to use the Community Hall for a play.

"What now?" asked Kipi. "I suppose that's the end of it."

"It does look like the end." Daniel had to agree with him this time. "The Church Hall won't have us, and now the Community Hall won't have us either. We can't put on a play just anywhere. We must have a stage."

"I'm not a bit sorry we can't use the Community Hall," said Debora, cheerfully. "It was too big. We couldn't put on a funny play there. Everyone would be too scared to laugh. We'll have to find somewhere else, that's all."

"But there isn't any other hall," shouted Kipi.

He had begun to believe in the project when they were practising at the Church Hall. Now he was so disappointed that it made him angry with everyone. Why were the girls refusing to see that the idea was finished?

"Then we'll have to think of somewhere else that isn't a hall," said Rachel.

"Huh!" said Kipi.

After a while he went on, "My brother's very angry about this. He won't mend the Caretaker's bicycle. It's been lying in his workshop since Saturday. The Caretaker keeps sending his children to ask when it will be ready. He's too ashamed to come himself. My brother is waiting for him!"

"It wasn't really the Caretaker's fault," said Debora. "I expect the Councillor made him do it."

"He should come and explain that to my brother," said Kipi. He was still looking fierce. "Then perhaps he may get his bicycle back. I don't think my brother is ever going to mend it."

"Perhaps Jacob's father can persuade the Caretaker to change his mind," suggested Rachel.

"No." Jacob shook his head. "I don't think that's a good idea. He may agree when my father asks him and then refuse at the last moment."

"Well, then, what can we do? Where else can we go? That's the end, I suppose," said Kipi again.

That's the question, thought Jacob. *Where else can we go?*

Chapter 8

That night Jacob thought a lot about what Rachel had said. *We'll have to think of somewhere else that isn't a hall*, she had said.

He did not want to believe that their hard work was going to be wasted. He did not want Sara to be disappointed. But where could they put the play on that was not a hall?

Another full moon was shining down on him as he lay on his bed, thinking hard. Time was passing quickly. Soon it would be the fifteenth. What could they do?

He was sure the Councillor was responsible for their first disappointment. As for the Community Hall, it was clear that he had persuaded the Council Secretary to refuse permission. Had that horrible man won at last? Jacob did not want to believe it.

When he arrived at school next day, he found Daniel and Kipi waiting. Their faces were very serious. He could see that they had not had any new ideas.

But when Rachel and Debora came in together, it was quite different. Both of them were smiling, and their steps were so light they nearly danced to their desks.

"You've thought of something," said Jacob. "What is it? Tell me!"

"Not now," Debora smiled. "You'll have to see it."

"Then let's go between lessons."

"No," they both said.

"What, then?"

"When school is over."

"Can't you just tell us what it is?"

"No."

So the boys had to wait, grumbling.

When school was over, Debora and Rachel led them up the path towards the games field.

"Look!"

"Look at what?"

"At the Principal's house."

They all looked.

The Principal's house was one of the oldest on the compound. It had been built in colonial times, before independence. There was a large central room with bedrooms at both ends. Behind the house was a separate kitchen and bathroom.

The main central room had one big doorway closed by two doors. In front of the doors was a very wide verandah with a roof over it. At each side cement pillars held up the roof. Flowering vines, pink and white, climbed round and round them. More flowering plants bordered the road, but there were spaces between the steps and the bushes nearest to them.

In front of the verandah a flight of five very wide steps led down to the road. Across the road was a gentle slope that led up to the edge of the games field.

"What about it?" asked Kipi.

"Don't you see?" said Rachel. "It looks like a stage."

"It looks like a house," said Kipi.

"No, *look!* The wide flat space in front of the doors is like a stage!"

"I suppose it could be . . ." began Daniel. He did not sound at all sure about it.

Kipi was quite sure. He shook his head firmly.

"You've done it!" shouted Jacob. "You've found the place!"

He ran down the slope and across the narrow road, then stood on the top step, turned and faced his friends.

"My people!" he began, in his Chief's voice. "Listen to me, my people."

The door behind him opened, and the Principal stood there.

"I'm listening, Jacob," she said smiling. "I suppose that's a speech from that play of yours. But why are you acting the play on my verandah?"

So they all went inside the house and sat down. Trying not to talk all at once, they told the Principal the story.

Of course, she knew most of it already. The teachers had talked about Sara and her eye trouble. They had told her how Sara's friends were trying to help. But she had not heard about their problems with the two halls. She began to feel angry when she heard that.

"So you think you can act your play outside on my verandah?"

"Yes – but only if you agree, Madam, of course."

"Yes. Of course. Let's go outside and look at it. I see it every day, you know. But I'd never thought of the verandah and steps as a stage before. Whose idea was this?"

"Rachel and Debora thought of it," said Jacob with a big smile.

They all went outside, looked, talked about it, and at last agreed. The Principal wrote down the dates of the performances, and when the practices would be.

The date for the first performance was getting very close.

"You'd better start telling everyone now," the Principal told them. "Tell people to bring mats or stools to sit on. We'll have a few chairs for older people, but young people and small children can sit on mats."

There was still a great deal to be done. Sara had to change some scenes yet again to fit the new stage. They had to think about the time of the performance, too.

"If we begin at six o'clock, it will be dark by the time we finish. Nobody will be able to see what's going on."

"We'll try to begin at five o'clock, but you know people will always come late. The dancing takes time. Then we have to make the collection for Sara. And the Principal wants to make a speech."

"So even if we start at five o'clock, it'll still be getting dark before we finish."

Rachel and Debora were still full of good ideas.

"Why don't we light bush lamps and put them along the walls on each side of the verandah? Nobody will notice them while it's daylight. As it gets dark, they'll light up the verandah and the top of the steps."

"What happens if one of the lamps starts to smoke?" asked Kipi.

"Whoever isn't on stage will have to watch the lamps. If one of them starts to smoke . . . well, just turn it out," Rachel explained.

"What if they all start to smoke?"

"Kipi!" they shouted. "Don't start again!"

Jacob's father looked for someone who was travelling to Sabah. He sent all the news to his journalist friend. He told him about the problems as well, and how they had solved the problem of a hall.

The journalist arranged to travel down to see the play for himself.

"I knew it!" he said to himself. "There's a story in this for me."

At last the great day came, and the first performance began. People came and sat down at the edge of the road, and on the slope of the field behind it. They brought chairs and mats.

Jacob put a line of white stones on the narrow road to keep a space for the dancers. Daniel cleaned every lamp until it shone like new. He lit each one and put it in place.

The Principal greeted them all, and the play began.

They like it, Jacob thought as he watched.

"They like it!" said Rachel and Debora, and they hugged each other as they waited to go out again on to the stage.

"They like it!" Kipi said to Daniel as they came off together. He sounded very surprised.

"Of course they do," said Daniel.

Halfway through the play, the little girls danced for the Chief and his guests. Jacob, Daniel and Kipi sat looking very important, until the dancers went away down the road. The audience clapped and cheered.

Then the Principal came out on to the stage again.

"Before we find out what happens next, I have something to say."

"Hush! Hush!" people said to each other.

The Principal made her little speech. "I'm sure all of you know why we're here. Sara has a problem with her eyes. If we want to save her from being blind for the rest of her life, we have to help her to go to the eye hospital in Sabah."

She looked around at the people, who were listening to every word.

"This play is acted by Sara's friends, to raise money for the journey. These young people have given all they have – their time and lots of hard work, to help their friend. Now it's your turn to give as much as you can. May God bless and reward you."

Kipi and Daniel left the stage and went round with plates. Nearly everyone put in some money. Then the play went on.

As the evening grew darker, people noticed the light from the lamps. It began to show itself like magic, lighting up the stage.

"Look at that!" they said to each other. "What a clever idea."

At the end of the play, the audience clapped and cheered again. They went on clapping for a long time. They did not want to go away. But at last they left. The actors were tired but very happy. They collected the chairs and swept the verandah. They could hear the talking and laughing as the people went home.

"They liked us!" smiled Rachel.

"There'll be more here tomorrow, you'll see." Daniel almost danced as he stacked the chairs.

"If it doesn't rain."

But everyone was too happy to take any notice of Kipi.

Before the third performance Jacob hurried down to see Sara. Everyone had told her all the news. But Jacob had another idea.

"Tomorrow, about this time, I'm coming to take you to the play. So be ready."

Sara shook her head. "I don't want to come. I can't see it."

"Of course you want to come. You can listen, can't you? Don't you want to hear how it sounds? We are wonderful!"

He put on his Chief's face and voice. Sara started to laugh.

"Mama Sara is coming with the young ones. I'll carry you on the bicycle. Sara, you must come."

So she agreed.

There were more people than ever. Some had come a second or third time and brought their friends. The Principal made her little speech, but this time she added something new.

"One other person must have some praise. I mean the one who wrote this play which we're all enjoying so much."

She went inside her house to where Sara was sitting. Before the girl could guess what was happening, the Principal led her out on to the stage.

"This is Sara, who wrote the play," she said.

The audience saw a thin young girl in an old dress. She was very clean and tidy. A head scarf was wrapped across her eyes.

"This is Sara," said the Principal again.

Sara knew everyone must be looking at her. She wanted to run away, but the Principal was holding her hand tightly.

She faced the shadows, full of unseen people. She smiled a little, bravely, and made her bow to them. People cheered and clapped and talked loudly to each other.

The Principal led Sara back inside and helped her to her chair.

"Now," she said to the others. "Get out there and collect some money. Then we have to get this audience quiet and finish the play."

"Thank you, Madam!" they said, and they hurried out with their plates.

When they came back, Jacob put on an angry look, threw his cloth over his shoulder and stamped out on to the stage.

"My people!" he shouted. "Listen to me, my people!"

It took a long time to get the people quiet. But at last cries of "Hush! Hush!" were heard. Slowly the talking stopped.

"My people! Listen to me!" said Jacob again, and the play went on for the last time to the very end.

Chapter 9

The next day the friends met in Jacob's house to talk about the money they had collected.

"Do you think it'll be enough?" Kipi asked anxiously.

"It has to be enough," said Daniel. "It's all we have, so it's all we can spend."

"What we collected is enough for the train fare," said Rachel. "And it will pay for two meals a day for one week, longer if they don't eat any meat."

"What about the other things they need to pay for?"

"Kipi!" everyone said angrily.

"But I'm right," he said firmly. "There are lots of other things to pay for. How will they get to the station to take the train? How will they get from the station to the hospital? Where will they stay in Sabah? What if they have to stay longer than a week?"

"Yes, Kipi, you're right," agreed Jacob. "We said there'd be other things to pay for, and there'll be some we haven't even thought about. But I can answer your questions, just the same."

He took a paper from his pocket. "People have been speaking to my father and the Principal. They're offering help. I think they were upset when they saw Sara last night. First, the man who owns the bus that passes the station will take Sara and her mother and make sure they get on the train safely."

"Oh, that's good!" said Rachel.

"Second, Papa's friend in Sabah has arranged for someone to meet them at the station and bring them to his home. Papa says his friend's wife is a very kind woman and they'll like her very much. She'll make sure they get to the hospital."

He looked around at the others, who were listening hard.

"If Sara has to stay in the hospital, Mama Sara may stay with her. But if not, they can both live with the journalist and his wife. That solves several problems – where to live and how to eat."

"That's so kind! We'll have to see him and thank him," Debora said.

"I'd like to see the photos he took," said Daniel. "The ones he took in the classroom were very funny."

"He's promised to send copies of everything. He left this morning for Sabah, to write his story – "

"What story?" asked Kipi.

"A story about the play, and Sara. For the newspaper. He kept saying there was a story here. Do you know, he'd already told the doctors about Sara and all we've been doing here in the village? She won't have to struggle to see them. He says they're waiting for her to come."

"That's wonderful! He's so kind," said Debora again.

"Everyone's talking about the play, my brother says," said Kipi. "When they come into his shed they sit down and talk about it."

Rachel thought he looked so happy she hardly knew him.

"We've started something," Jacob agreed. "Now all we have to do is to get Sara and her mother on that train as soon as we can."

At the school, the Principal was meeting the teachers. They talked about the play and congratulated each other for having such students in the school.

Then the Principal said, "Our young people now have enough money for two return tickets on the popular side of the train. But as we all know that side is so crowded. People squeeze inside. You can't find anywhere to sit down, except on someone's bag of goods."

The teachers laughed.

"It won't be easy for Mama Sara. She's never travelled anywhere before. And it'll be really frightening for Sara because she can't see what's going on."

Everyone agreed. "Two days like that . . . yes, it will be very hard for them. And what about food?"

"You know what happens. When the train gets to the station, people rush out and buy food from the traders. Then the bell rings and everyone rushes back into the train. Sara and her mother won't be able to do that."

Again the teachers agreed. "That's how thieves steal a lot of things."

"Must they go by train?" one of the teachers asked. "It would be much quicker to go by road. The train is so slow."

"I thought of that," said the Principal. "But it will cost much more money. They'd have to change buses three or four times, too. And buses break down on the road sometimes. At least in the train they can go all the way without changing. I'm told that someone will see that they get on safely. And someone is meeting them in Sabah."

"Then I suggest," said Mr Buah, "that we make a gift so that they can reserve first class tickets. They'll have a part of the train for themselves where they can rest, their own small room."

"What a good idea," the Principal said. It was what she had hoped someone would say.

"If we have a little extra," another teacher added, "we can give something to one of the staff on the train to make sure they get some food."

The teachers were not the only group who were talking about Sara. The women held a special meeting to talk about Sara, her family and their problem.

"Does this girl have no members of her family who can help her? We know her mother well. We see her in the market or going to farm every day. We know that she's a widow, but her husband had a brother."

"Is the Councillor's wife here?" asked the President. "No? Write down her name. She'll have to pay a fine. Yes, the Councillor is the husband's brother. What is he doing about this?"

After some talk, they decided to ask the men to talk to the Councillor.

"But Mama Sara and her daughter must travel soon," others said. "We can't wait for the men to do something. You heard what the Principal said."

"It's true that our children have collected some money for them. But there'll be many things they haven't thought about. It isn't easy for the mother of a young family to travel a long way, and leave the children behind. We don't want Mama Sara to feel worried while she's in that strange place."

They decided to give some money to buy soap and a new pair of slippers. One woman promised to send her two grown-up daughters to look after the younger children. Other women promised to give the family some food.

The President said that she would lend Mama Sara two wrappers, blouses and a new head tie. The Vice President sold second-hand clothes in the market. She promised to find two dresses to fit Sara.

A few women said that all this giving was too much, but the President was firm.

"How many of us have been to Sabah? If Mama Sara and her daughter go there in rags, what will the women of Sabah say about our village and those who live here? It will be a great shame to us."

"The children have shown us the way," the Vice President agreed. "It's late. But it's not too late to help this girl and her mother."

They began to talk about the play then, and to praise the mothers of the actors and the dancers.

"But why did they show the play on the edge of a field?" someone asked. "It would be better in the Church Hall next time."

"Is the Caretaker's wife here?" asked the President. "No? Write down her name. She has to pay a fine next time. I heard they asked the Caretaker to let them use the Hall. He said 'yes'. Then later he said 'no'."

"Aaah!" they said.

"Why did he say 'no'?" asked the Vice President. "That's another question we'll pass on to the men. The children showed the play on the edge of the field because there was nowhere else to go."

"Aaah!" the women said again, looking at each other.

The women who had promised to help went to see Mama Sara. When she heard what they had to say, she did not know whether to laugh or cry.

Sara's friends were visiting her, and they came out to thank the mothers.

"Good people! Good people!" said Mama Sara. "You've all done so well. What shall I do with the young children? What about the goat? Oh Sara! This is your chance if the doctors can help you. Perhaps my sister can come. So I am to go in a train. What is a train? How can I go to Sabah? Where is Sabah?"

"Mama Sara, you said you'd go to the moon," Jacob reminded her.

"Oh yes, I'll go," she said. "I've seen the moon. It doesn't look far if I could get up there. I've never seen Sabah."

Quite a big crowd of people came to the road side to see Sara and her mother start their trip. Everything had been arranged. The small bus would take them to the station. The owner and the driver, both dressed well for such an important occasion, would see they got safely on the train. Their places had already been reserved.

Sara and her mother climbed up the steps and sat down on the worn plastic seats. The driver started the engine with a roar and a cloud of smoke.

"Safe journey!"

The two travellers waved their hands. With another roar the bus began to move. Sara's brothers and sisters did not know whether to jump up and down because they were excited, or cry because they were being left behind. Everyone waved and watched until the bus was out of sight.

"We did it!" said Kipi. "I always knew we would."

"Kipi!" everyone shouted.

Nobody knew how long the travellers would be away, so everyone was ready to wait. But a few days later there was something new to talk about. The journalist's story appeared in the *News of the Nation* on Sunday.

Jacob's father called Jacob to look at it when a copy reached the village after a few days.

Friendship, it read. *Can Sara's sight be saved? Her friends have done everything to get this girl from a remote village to the doctors!*

The whole story was there with all the problems they had solved. There were photos – the first practices in the classroom, and the last performance. There was a very good one of Sara being led out to face the audience.

There was a marked lack of help from those who could and should have helped, the story went on. *But nothing could deter Sara's friends. They acted their play on the steps of a house when they were refused the use of the Church Hall normally used for social events . . .*

"I wonder how many people have seen this," Jacob said.

"What do you think of it?"

"It makes it sound more wonderful than it was. We just wanted to help. I think it blames some people. It'll make readers ask what other people were doing. And look at that bit about the Church Hall!"

"Exactly."

"I think everyone's going to hear about this story."

"That's what the journalist hopes every time he writes one."

Chapter
10

At first the friends counted the days. They looked at the map and followed the route of the railway line north.

"If it takes two days, then this morning they should be *here*."

Next day they told each other, "They're in Sabah now."

And next day, "I expect they're just going to the hospital."

After that they did not know what was happening. There was no news until the owner of the bus brought another copy of the newspaper from the station. He now felt he was an important part of the whole project.

There was a photo of Sara and her mother in the newspaper. They were standing on the steps of the hospital.

"Is that pretty woman Mama Sara?" said Rachel. They hardly knew her in her borrowed wrapper and blouse, and her new head tie.

After that there was no news for some time.

In the village people were still talking about the newspaper story which the journalist had written.

"This is a shame to us. We did nothing. When our children wanted to help, someone tried to stop them."

The Councillor became unpopular. If people met him, they greeted him. That was the custom. But when he went past on his motor bike, people no longer waved and shouted his name.

The Caretaker also had a bad time. Kipi's brother still had his bicycle. The women asked his wife what her husband had been doing.

"He said the play wasn't suitable."

"That's not true," the President said, and the others agreed. "We all saw that play. There was no trouble in it."

The men's meeting called the Caretaker up to explain. One of the men shook a newspaper at him.

"Those who could have helped did nothing, or made problems for the children. That's what it says here, in the newspaper. Now everyone's asking what kind of people live in this place. It's a shame to us."

"And then," Jacob's father told him later, "the Caretaker admitted that the Councillor had told him to do it. He was too afraid to refuse. People are going to remember this. Even if nothing else happens, the Councillor is going to find it harder to be elected next time."

"If nothing else happens . . . What do you mean?" asked Jacob.

His father laughed. "My son, you're too quick. Let that one rest for a while."

The third week began. The bus owner called with the news that Sara and her mother would be coming back on the Saturday train.

"Is there any news about her eyes?" asked Debora anxiously.

The bus owner shook his head. "Nothing, I'm afraid."

"Oh, I can't bear it!" sighed Rachel. "Saturday is so far away. Why didn't they tell us what happened?"

On Saturday the train was late. A little crowd of people waited patiently at the roadside. Every time a cloud of dust told them that something was coming, everyone got up. But that something was never the bus. So when it had passed everyone sat down again. At last the small bus appeared. It stopped with a roar and a cloud of smoke, the same as it had started.

Mama Sara came down the step. She looked round, saw the friends, and smiled and waved.

Then Sara came down. She was wearing dark glasses. But she too looked around, saw them, *saw them*, and waved.

They waved back, wildly.

"She saw us?" asked Kipi.

"She saw us," said Jacob.

"She saw us!" the others shouted. They danced about, waving their hands.

The owner of the bus told everyone how long he had waited at the station. The driver, smiling when he saw how excited everyone was, brought out the travelling bags.

Sara's brothers and sisters were jumping up and down, waiting their turn to hug her and hug their mother. The friends rushed over and joined them.

"Sara, can you see now?" everyone was asking.

"Yes, I can see."

"Why are you wearing those dark glasses?" Kipi wanted to know.

"They protect my eyes from the strong sunlight," she explained. "It won't be for long – about three months."

They picked up the bags. They thanked the men in the bus and started back along the path to Sara's house.

The goat was in her pen, pulling down fresh leaves from the bundle tied to the pole. She looked well-fed and healthy.

The hens were scratching around near their house. They all looked fine, and one had six small chicks.

"Oh, it's so good to be back. Now I must make some food."

"Sit down, Mama Sara. There's food ready in the kitchen."

Sara had taken off her dark glasses and put on a clear pair. Her eyes were bright and shining.

"Look at Sara helping Debora and Rachel," said Mama Sara. "Isn't it wonderful to see her moving about again?"

She sighed happily. "I have so much to tell you. So much! I'll still be telling you new things next year. Those people! So kind! And you, my children. God alone can reward you. Sara can see again, and the doctors think she won't have any more problems."

Next day, Mama Sara put on her old clothes, washed the borrowed clothes and ironed them neatly with the charcoal iron. Then she went round the villages.

First she had to return the borrowed clothes. But the President told her to keep the scarf and slippers.

Next she called on the parents of the actors and the dancers. Then she called on everyone who had been to see the play and given some money.

She gave out some sweets. The people in Sabah had given her many packets of sweets as gifts.

Everyone wanted to know all about the trip, about the city, the hospital, what the doctors had done for Sara. They wanted to know everything – how much things cost, where they stayed, what they ate. There was no end to the questions. It took Mama Sara a long time to answer all of them. But she enjoyed herself very much.

Sara told her own story at school. She went to thank the teachers and the Principal.

"I made so many friends there. I met some girls like me in hospital. We're going to write and keep in touch."

"I know a little poem, Sara," said the Principal. "It goes like this:
>Make a lot of new friends
>Remember still the old,
>New friends are of silver,
>Old friends are of gold."

"Yes," said Sara. "I know what that means."

Everyone hoped that Sara would be allowed to join them in class. But that was not possible. She had missed too many lessons.

"I don't mind," she told them. "I'm so happy to be back in school. I'll be a Mama to those young ones in our old class."

So the friends helped her with the work she had missed. Slowly everyone settled down once again to the peaceful life of the village.

But that was not quite the end of the story.

Mama Sara went to the next women's meeting. She knew everyone wanted to hear again about her travels. She answered everyone's questions happily.

When everyone was satisfied, the President moved on to something else.

"Now, Mama Sara, tell us, if you will, something about that piece of farm land by the river . . ."

A few months later, a group of men went to see the Councillor. He was quite used to people coming to ask for help, or to settle a quarrel.

They explained who they were, and slowly the Councillor began to feel worried. These were men who had gone out to work in towns.

But first they talked about the weather and the crops, the state of the village, the road, and other important things. Then the eldest spoke.

"We all heard about this girl Sara and her trouble. We saw her photo in the newspaper. We know her mother. We read the name of our own village. We wonder why that family has nobody to help them."

There was silence.

"And we wonder about the big piece of land by the river. Why are you farming there?"

"Everything that belonged to my brother now belongs to me," said the Councillor boldly. "I had . . . er . . . lent him that piece of land."

"Then why don't you look after his family?" asked one of the men. "As for the land, your brother had that land from me. He told me his wife gave him the money for it."

There was silence.

"It's time to let that old quarrel rest," the eldest went on. "In the next world, do you know if your mother and her co-wife are now good friends? Perhaps that's why you couldn't stop Jacob from helping your brother's child."

The Councillor did not know what to say.

"Give back the land. Do you agree? Perhaps the villages will forgive you . . . before the elections come."

"Very well, I agree."

"Let's go straight to Mama Sara and tell her."

She was sitting outside in the moonlight with her children, telling stories. As the men came up the path, they could hear the laughing and clapping. The children were singing the little song that came in the story at that point.

Everyone sat down and talked about the weather, the crops and Sara's health. Then the men looked at the Councillor and waited.

"Mama Sara," he began. He did not want to go on.

The men looked at him very hard.

"Er . . ." he went on. "I find I made a mistake. The land by the river doesn't belong to me. I am giving it back to you."

"At once," someone added.

"At once," he said.

"With all the crops I've planted on it."

"With all those crops."

"Everything is yours. I have no right to it."

The men told him what to say. He said the words after them.

"And these men are all my witnesses."

"All witnesses!"

"So that's where the story really ends," Jacob's father told his friend the journalist. He had come to take photos of Sara back in school, to finish his own story for the newspaper. The Principal sat with them on her verandah.

"Look at them all coming now," she said. "Sara's there . . . do you see her?" She called to them: "Where are you all going?"

"We want to ask Kipi's brother to give the Caretaker his bicycle," Jacob called back to them.

"Jacob is a fine son of his father," the journalist said.

The Principal added, "And Sara has golden friends."

Already available in **Mactracks**

Starters

The Hunter's Dream Meja Mwangi
More than anything, the hunter wishes for a child. In a strange and wonderful way, his dream comes true. But can this dream last in the real world?

Martha's Mistakes Lorna Evans
The delightful story of one little girl who tries hard to be helpful, but . . . Martha never quite gets the result she planned.

Fiki Learns to Like Other People Lauretta Ngcobo
Fiki finds out the hard way that being unkind to others does not make you happy inside.

Zulu Spear Olive Langa
A story of bravery and courage in battle, set in the time of King Cetshwayo and the Zulu wars against the British.

Mercy in a Hurry Mary Harrison
A busy market presents problems for Mercy as she tries to hurry through it to meet her father by four o'clock.

Tanzai and Bube John Haynes
Bube is the local bully, but he is no match for clever little Tanzai.

Sprinters

Mystery of the Sagrenti Treasure Ekow Yarney
In this exciting adventure story, Kofi and his friends are on the trail of a British soldier's hidden treasure, looted in the Asante wars over one hundred years ago. But are they alone in their search?

Eyes and Ears Brenda Ferry
The theft of a local art treasure is a puzzle for Ike, Obi, Emeka and Chinwe to solve, through their secret group, Eyes and Ears.

Eyes and Ears Work Hard Brenda Ferry
Trouble again for the four friends as they try to solve the mystery of the disappearing market trader and his beautiful lace cloth.

One in a Million Emma Johnson
When Simon finds a winning lottery ticket, he sees it as a way of solving his family's problems. But he must travel many miles to claim the ticket prize, and there is no time to spare.

Map on the Wall Colin Swatridge
Two young boys have to outwit a gang of kidnappers in this fast-moving adventure story set in Sierra Leone.

Magic Trees Jenny Vincent
All trees are magic, as Chido and Tambu find out when they step inside the hollow tree and are whirled away on a journey through time and space. What they see teaches them a few things they will never forget – that is, if they ever get home again!

Runners

Guitar Wizard Walije Gondwe
Set in Britain and Malawi, this is the true story of Wezi, a Malawian boy growing up in London. Wezi's greatest wish is to make music, and he is determined to make his dream come true.

Star Nandi Dlovu
Tanka, a modern independent girl, tries to prevent her friend Star from being trapped by the traditions of village life. But she soon finds she has a fight on her hands.

Days of Silence Rosina Umelo
Suddenly something is very wrong in the country, and everyone is on the move. Four children find themselves quite alone, and have to work out how to survive through the difficult days of a coup.

Never Leave Me Hope Dube
Mary thinks she is in love, and will not listen to the advice of her friend Agnes. Is Peter as wonderful as he seems, or is Mary just heading for trouble?

Juwon's Battle Victor Thorpe
Juwon has to take on the suspicions of local people and the power of an evil chief, in order to rescue her little brother and save her grandmother's good name.

Winners

Halima Meshack Asare
At first Halima finds everything is new and exciting in the city. But soon, things begin to change, and her desert home village seems very far away. She has to make some difficult and dangerous decisions.

Foli Fights the Forgers Kofi Quaye
A day out in Accra turns into a nightmare for young Foli Kwansa as he stumbles across a gang of currency forgers.

Presents from Mr Bakare Mary Harrison
Set in Lagos, this story uncovers a spider's web of money, drugs and danger. Femi has to protect himself and his sister against all odds.

Sara's Friends Rosina Umelo
Sara has a serious eye disease and she needs help to save her sight. Her friends have to find a way of raising the money, but how? And not everybody wants to help . . .

Trouble in the City Hope Dube
Juma helps out at the supermarket in the Megacity shopping centre. His sharp eyes don't miss much. Who are the two suspicious looking strangers hanging around the bank opposite? Juma decides to find out.

Be Beautiful Lydia Eagle and Barbara Jackson *(non-fiction)*
An information book packed with useful ideas on beauty care to help every teenage girl look her best – without spending lots of money!

Sport in Africa Ossie Stuart *(non-fiction)*
A fresh look at sport in Africa, past and present. Modern sports including football and athletics are highlighted, together with some famous sporting personalities, and the excitement of national and international competition.